PRACTICA...

Study Guide for Power Healing

PRACTICAL HEALING

Study Guide for Power Healing

John Wimber
and
Kevin Springer

HODDER AND STOUGHTON
LONDON SYDNEY AUCKLAND TORONTO

British Library Cataloguing in Publication Data
Wimber, John
    Practical healing: study guide for power healing.
    1. Spiritual healing
    I. Title   II. Springer, Kevin
    615.8'52   BT732.5

ISBN 0 340 41850 8

*Hodder and Stoughton Editorial Office: 47 Bedford Square, London WC1B
3DP.*

Contents

Introduction: How to use this study guide   7

Session 1: Why divine healing?   15

Session 2: Suffering   23

Session 3: Healing the whole person   31

Session 4: Overcoming the effects of past hurts   37

Session 5: Healing the demonised   47

Session 6: Healing the body   55

Session 7: An integrated model of healing   61

Session 8: A healing procedure, part 1   69

Session 9: A healing procedure, part 2   75

Session 10: A healing lifestyle   79

Appendix A: Tips for leaders   85

Appendix B: Sources for chapter readings   91

Introduction: How to use this study guide

Three years ago a group of ten people from a church that I (Kevin Springer) pastored attended John Wimber's healing seminar in Detroit, Michigan. During the three-day seminar many of their questions about divine healing were answered, they saw others effectively pray for the sick, they prayed for the sick themselves, and, in several instances, they were prayed over for a ministry of healing. Almost every one of these ten people said it was one of the most significant experiences of his or her Christian life. On returning home the group asked me what they should do next.

The group was composed of ordinary people: mothers, a meter reader, a dentist, a factory worker, a student, and a salesman (the group's leader) – all faithful Christians united only by a desire to serve God and his people more fully. But I saw in these people a source of healing and renewal for the entire congregation, so I suggested they meet weekly to learn about divine healing and be available to pray for the sick. They eagerly took up my suggestion, and a 'healing team' was formed.

At first the group was content to listen to John Wimber's

audio teaching tapes on divine healing. While the tapes were quite helpful, members of the team also wanted written material that would accomplish two goals: answer tough questions about divine healing and teach them how to pray for the sick.

We often receive enquiries from people wanting to learn about literature that contains a comprehensive introduction to divine healing *and* practical suggestions for how to pray. We designed this study guide to fill that need.

VARIETY OF GROUPS

We wrote this book with a variety of small groups in mind: Sunday school classes, interdenominational Bible study groups, fellowship gatherings, charismatic prayer groups and church service teams.

Pastoral approval, support and involvement is necessary for a local church small group to become a source of broader congregational renewal. So we recommend that small groups considering this study first talk with their pastors to seek their approval. If pastors cannot participate in the group study, we encourage on-going dialogue to avoid any misunderstanding or conflict in the congregation and to demonstrate appropriate honour and respect for pastoral authority.

We have several group-oriented goals in mind for this study guide. First, it is an aid for individual study, helping to highlight key issues raised in *Power Healing* and stimulate thought and prayer. Second, it is a guide to group discussion about issues raised in the book. A by-product of this discussion is the inspiration and motivation to pray for the sick. Third, it is a manual from which participants may learn how to pray for the sick effectively.

To achieve these three goals we developed ten sessions, each session containing five parts and an annotated list of books for further study.

The *purpose statements* at the beginning of each session inform the participant about what he or she should expect to learn. Pay close attention to these statements; we have worded them carefully. Usually the goal has two parts, gaining understanding about some topic (such as suffering or inner healing) and learning a new skill (such as how to conduct a diagnostic interview).

The introductory *readings* from other sources expand on the topics found in *Power Healing*. We chose them to inspire thought and discussion, not necessarily to provide new information.

The *daily scripture readings* foster both contemplation about God's truth and personal prayer. We encourage you to look up each passage of scripture and to use a good study Bible, utilising its cross-reference system, study notes and concordance. (We relied on *The NIV Study Bible* in the writing of *Power Healing*, and highly recommend it to you too.)

PRAYER, DISCUSSION, CLINIC

The ten small-group sessions are most effectively covered in weekly meetings. More frequent gatherings will deny crucial individual study and prayer time; less frequent meetings will frustrate and discourage those eager to pray for the sick.

We recommend that the meeting times be broken up into three parts, each lasting about thirty minutes. The most important part of the meeting is *worship and prayer*. Worship creates a healing environment, the Holy Spirit's presence and faith for healing. In the ninth chapter of *Power Healing* we write: 'There are actions that we can take which increase faith for healing. The most significant is worship. As we draw close to God his Spirit works in us. Because church gatherings [including small groups] include open, corporate worship, they can be powerful environments for healing.'

It is neither our place nor our desire to dictate a particular style of worship for your group; that is best determined by your particular denominational tradition. God sees and recognises the attitude of your heart, that inner disposition of surrender and thanksgiving that may be expressed in exuberant singing, contemplative prayer or faithful liturgy. Small-group prayer and worship generally works well when a trained musician (a guitar or piano player) leads the group in singing. Regardless of your worship style, we encourage you to invite the Holy Spirit to come among you, teach you and release his healing power in you during the gathering.

The second part of the meeting is *discussion* based on the questions provided in this guide. As we wrote the questions we kept in mind a Persian proverb: 'It is harder to ask a sensible question than to supply a sensible answer.' We think 'sensible questions' for the purposes of small groups are discussion *starters* only, and they are intended to elicit other questions related to each topic. Many of the questions will point participants back to the book, forcing them to reread key sections carefully. Other questions will raise issues not discussed in the book. In both instances the goal is to stimulate thoughtful discussion and not to encourage the regurgitation of clichés.

The key ingredient of a successful discussion is a gifted leader, a person who brings out the best in others without dominating the discussion. We do not believe the leader must be a great teacher or a 'healing answer man'. Another element of successful discussions is that each participant has reviewed the questions before each session, so that he or she can contribute thoughtful insights.

The last part of the meeting is the *clinic*. The gifting and skills of leaders determine the success or failure of clinics. The most effective leaders are those who themselves have been trained to pray for the sick. However, in many instances trained leaders are not available. So, beyond practical experience, what qualities are required for effective clinic leaders? Perhaps the most important is the *willingness to take risks*, to step out in faith relying on the Spirit's leading to heal the sick. Closely related to this is *perseverance*, a steady persistence in praying even in the face of failure. Another important quality is *teachableness*, the ability to receive correction and instruction from others. (For more on leadership, see 'Appendix A: Tips for leaders' at the back of this volume.)

For many people, the clinics are quite threatening, even frightening. Do not be alarmed by this. Praying for the sick is like personal evangelism, scripture study or any other exercise in the Christian life: it requires understanding, good examples and personal practice for success. All of this takes time. Throughout the ten sessions you will grow in confidence and ease in praying for the sick, and many of you will either be healed or see others healed through your prayers.

SPECTATOR, PARTICIPANT, TRAINER

We have observed several stages through which people pass in learning how to pray for the sick. In the first stage they are *spectators* – listening, observing and evaluating others who know how to pray for the sick. Frequently they are personally healed or observe someone whom they know receive healing. These personal experiences, combined with teaching or discussion about healing, inspire and motivate them to learn how to pray for the sick.

The next stage is becoming *participants*; that is, they cease being spectators and begin to pray for the sick. They first pray only in healing clinics, where they receive help and guidance from others. But in time, as they grow in confidence, they are willing to pray for the sick away from Christian gatherings. For these people, healing is a part of the normal Christian life, like scripture study, personal evangelism or prayer.

Many who participate in this ten-week study will become participants, people who actually pray for the sick. In fact this is the primary purpose for writing the guide, that you might believe in and be a vehicle of God's healing power.

There are some people, a minority to be sure, who are called and gifted for a third stage of the divine healing ministry. They become *trainers*, or equippers, men and women who through word and deed will train others to pray for the sick. The healing team that we mentioned at the beginning of this introduction had several members who became effective trainers. Their training ministry, under the leader's direction and encouragement, spread the healing ministry throughout the congregation.

A ten-week study is insufficient time to train equippers. Nevertheless, a few of you will sense that God is calling you to train others. We encourage you to continue praying for the sick, to study other books about healing (we provide extensive annotated bibliographies for this purpose) and, most significantly, to attend healing seminars and conferences where you can learn from others with more experience.

Our hope is that this guide will inspire you to pray for the sick. If as a result of this study only one person is healed because of your prayers, we will have fulfilled our purpose.

John Wimber
Kevin Springer
April 1987
Yorba Linda, California

Session 1: Why divine healing?

In *Power Healing*, read the Introduction, chapters 1–3 and Appendix D.

PURPOSE

Some people have never seriously considered the possibility that God can heal the sick today. Others have strong opinions for and against divine healing, feelings they have never expressed to others. Still others have perplexing questions about topics such as suffering or the supernatural for which they have never received adequate answers. Why is divine healing important?

READINGS

A purpose for sickness

The whole purpose of pain and suffering in nature is good; it's to call our attention to something that is wrong with us, so that we can do something about it and get rid of it. When I'm sick, the pain concentrates my attention on my body or emotions until I do something to get rid of the sickness. The suffering and pain are good in that they center my efforts on getting rid of the sickness which is evil and is harming me.

Francis MacNutt

Divine healing: a touchstone of spiritual life

In spite of the cold and conservative, and sometimes scornful unbelief of many, this doctrine [of divine healing] is becoming one of the touchstones of the character and spiritual life in all the churches of America, and is revolutionizing, by a deep, quiet, and Divine movement, the whole Christian life of thousands. It has a profound bearing upon the spiritual life. No one can truly receive it without being a holier and more useful Christian.

A. B. Simpson

The gifts and the church

A church where the charismatic gifts in all their variety and wonder are not in evidence is something less than the church founded at Pentecost.

Donald Bloesch

DAILY SCRIPTURE READINGS

   Sunday: Moses prays for Miriam / Numbers 12:1–16
   Monday: The waters of Marah and Elim / Exodus 15:22–27
   Tuesday: Jesus and John the Baptist / Luke 7:18–35
Wednesday: Jesus heals many / Mark 1:14–34

Thursday: Jesus heals a paralytic / Matthew 9:1–8
Friday: The great commission / Mark 16:9–20
Saturday: The new Jerusalem / Revelation 21:1–8

DISCUSSION SESSION

The goal of the discussion session is to introduce the participants to the book *Power Healing* and the structure of the ten-week group study sessions, and to take time individually to answer the discussion questions.

The leader should introduce the main topics covered in the book *Power Healing*, describe the structure of the sessions (worship, discussion, clinic), and discuss what is expected in weekly preparation.

After a period of worship and prayer, take five minutes to individually review these discussion questions, indicating whether you agree or disagree with each statement. The purpose of these questions is not to harmonise your answers with the book's teaching; it is to help you form an opinion about divine healing. So be prepared to discuss your answer.

Discussion questions

1 The introduction says Jesus wants all Christians today to pray for the sick (see Mark 1:34; 16:18; Luke 9:1; 10:9). Do you agree or disagree?

2 The authors claim that if they pray for a hundred people and only one is healed the effort is worth it. Do you agree or disagree?

3 Many people draw hasty negative conclusions about divine healing, usually based on one bad personal experience. Do you agree or disagree?

4 Some people equate divine healing with New Age movement practices like psychic healing. Do you agree or disagree?

5 It is possible to acknowledge that supernatural healings occur in non-Christian contexts (that is, that evil spirits may sometimes heal for evil purposes) without denying divine healing. Do you agree or disagree?

6 Materialism and rationalism, two philosophies that influence our Western world-view, inhibit many Christians from believing in divine healing. Do you agree or disagree?

7 The authors believe that the demonstration of Christ's compassion and mercy is one of the primary purposes of divine healing. Do you agree or disagree?

8 Miracles like divine healings are subordinate and inferior to having faith in Christ. Do you agree or disagree?

9 Many Western Christians equate suffering with sickness, rather than persecution, because they are unaccustomed to persecution on account of the gospel. Do you agree or disagree?

10 Personal sin can lead to sickness. Do you agree or disagree?

11 Through healing the sick Jesus defeated Satan and demonstrated his superior rule. Do you agree or disagree?

12 Because the fullness of the kingdom of God has not yet come, the healing ministry is partial, already present in this age but not yet completed. Do you agree or disagree?

13 Divine healing touches every aspect of our lives: forgiveness of sin, restoration from sickness, breaking the hold of poverty and oppressive social structures, deliverance from demonic power and influence, and raising the dead. Do you agree or disagree?

14 The private sins of individuals may lead to sickness among members of a larger group of which they are members. Do you agree or disagree?

15 One of the most compelling reasons to pray for the sick is that Jesus, our example of faith and practice, healed many. Do you agree or disagree?

16 Because God is all-loving and all-powerful, it makes sense that he wants to heal the sick today. Do you agree or disagree?

17 Christians are called to pray for the sick in the same way that they are called to evangelise the lost. Do you agree or disagree?

18 Most people are hesitant, even fearful, about praying for others' healing because they misunderstand God's compassion and mercy. Do you agree or disagree?

19 In praying for the sick the Christian's part is to obey, pray, and rely on God's sovereign mercy; God's part is to heal. Do you agree or disagree?

CLINIC

The purpose of the clinic is to help the participants form an opinion about divine healing.

The larger group should be broken up into groups consisting of three people. Take about thirty minutes to discuss their answers to the questions. At the end of this time, while still in groups of three, ask if there is anyone who needs prayer for sickness. Pray for his or her healing (a simple prayer like 'Lord, heal [Janet] of her cold' will do), then you are dismissed.

SUGGESTED BOOKS FOR FURTHER STUDY

Bosworth, F. F. *Christ the Healer*. Old Tappan, NJ: Fleming H. Revell, 1973. (A series of sermons on healing from a famous early twentieth-century evangelist and healer.)

Brown, Colin. *That You May Believe*. Grand Rapids, MI: William B. Eerdmans, 1985. (An apologetic for miracles today, written by a seminary professor.)

Gardner, Rex. *Healing Miracles*. London: Darton, Longman and Todd, 1986. (The author, a Christian medical doctor, examines healing. The book is well written, with excellent medical and theological insights. We recommend this to Christians who are sceptical about divine healing.)

Gordon, A. J. *The Ministry of Healing*. Harrisburg, PA: Christian Publications, 1961. (This classic on healing, originally published in 1882, was written by the Baptist founder of Gordon College, an evangelical college in Massachusetts.)

Groothuis, Douglas R. *Unmasking the New Age*. Downers Grove, IL: InterVarsity Press, 1986. (The finest Christian introduction to the New Age Movement on the market today; the author, an instructor at the McKenzie Study Center in Eugene, Oregon, presents the topic in a responsible fashion.)

Lewis, C. S. *Miracles*. London: Collins Fount Books, 1977. (An apologetic for Christian miracles, first published in 1947.)

Martin, George. *Healing*. Ann Arbor, MI: Servant Books, 1977. (A simple and short [64 pages] introduction to divine healing for Roman Catholics.)

Martin, Trevor. *Kingdom Healing*. London: Marshalls, 1981. (The author argues from scripture that healing the sick confirms the preaching of the kingdom of God, and that God wants to heal today. This book gives a solid theological and biblical basis for divine healing.)

Milingo, E. *The World In Between*. New York: Orbis Books, 1984. (The author is the former Roman Catholic Bishop of Lusaka, Zambia. He tells how he began praying for the sick and casting out demons from people. This is an especially helpful book for understanding how worldviews affect theology. A most interesting and enlightening book.)

Neal, Emily Gardiner. *The Healing Ministry*. New York: Crossroad Books, 1985. (This is a personal journal written by an Episcopal deaconess who has conducted healing missions throughout the United States and Canada. A variety of topics are dealt with from a personal, devotional perspective.)

Osborn, T. L. *Healing the Sick*. Tulsa, OK: Harrison House, 1977. (A book on healing by one of the more popular practitioners today.)

Sanford, Agnes. *The Healing Light*. Evesham, Worcs: Arthur James, 1969. (The classic book of this century on divine healing.)

Idem. *The Healing Power of the Bible*. New York: Trumpet Books, 1969. (The author's thesis is that if miracles happened frequently in the Old and New Testaments, they can happen today.)

Schlemon, Barbara Leahy. *Healing Prayer*. Notre Dame, IN: Ave Maria Press, 1979. (A good introduction to divine healing for Roman Catholics.)

Seybold, Klaus, Ulrich B. Mueller. *Sickness and Healing*. Trans. by Douglas W. Stott. Nashville, TN: Abingdon Press, 1978. (The authors are German theologians who explore healing in the Old and New Testaments. It is a complete survey of healing in the Bible. Their conclusion, in this scholarly work, is that the Bible encountered sickness as a theological rather than a physical problem and that healing is actually the overcoming of suffering.)

Simpson, A. B. *The Gospel of Healing*. Harrisburg, PA: Christian Publications, 1915. (A surprising testimony in favour of divine healing by the founder of The Christian and Missionary Alliance church.)

Sipley, Richard M. *Understanding Divine Healing*. Wheaton, IL: Victory Books, 1986. (An introduction to divine healing written by a Christian and Missionary Alliance pastor from Saskatchewan, Canada.)

Wilson, Jim. *Healing Through the Power of Christ*. Cambridge: James Clarke & Co., Ltd., 1946. (This short book is an excellent introduction to healing prayer.)

Session 2: Suffering

In *Power Healing*, read pages 33–39 and chapter 8.

PURPOSE

To consider difficult questions about suffering and why some people are not healed when prayed for, and to learn how to pray for the sick with childlike faith.

READINGS

Take courage

We have not to make ourselves better in order to be healed, either spiritually or physically. Therefore let the sufferer take courage and lift up his weary head. O, ye unnumbered subjects of pain and bodily torture, with hands and feet which you would use so diligently and swiftly in the service of the Lord if they were only released from the fetters which bind them! O, ye countless victims of pain and disorder, who have never consecrated either your souls or your bodies to the service of him who made them, hear all of you that voice of him who speaketh from heaven, saying, 'I am the Lord that healeth thee.'

A. J. Gordon

Sovereignty

Is there an answer to the problem of human suffering? God does not answer all our questions any more than he answered Job's anguished cries. Rather, he reveals himself in all his love and sovereignty to our suffering hearts and points us through the cross of Christ to our destiny of glory. There is God's answer to our suffering. In that glorious hope our trusting souls may rest.

Margaret Clarkson

Suffering and sickness

It is clear that there is value in suffering, but the New Testament description of suffering does not include sickness. Whatever value there is in sickness was never urged upon the innumerable people ministered to in the Scripture narrative. In no case did it limit the availability of their healing in response to faith.

Jim Glennon

Making sense out of suffering

Jesus came, but he was not recognized by all, because he demanded faith. Instead of the spectacular visible triumph people expected, he showed himself only to those whose hearts (not just minds and eyes) were on the lookout for him.

It is the same today. Jesus' solution to the problem of suffering is available only to faith. Use that key and you enter an incredible new world of joy and meaning; rely only on reason or feeling or sight and you will not enter.

Peter Kreeft

DAILY SCRIPTURE READINGS

Sunday: David as a godly sufferer / Psalm 22 (also see Matthew 27:46)
Monday: The suffering servant / Isaiah 52:13–53:12
Tuesday: Jesus made like his brothers / Hebrews 2:5–18
Wednesday: Hope in suffering / 1 Peter 1:3–12
Thursday: Suffering for being a Christian / 1 Peter 4:1–19
Friday: Encouragement to be faithful / 2 Timothy 2:1–13
Saturday: More than conquerors / Romans 8:18–39

DISCUSSION SESSION

The goal of the discussion session is to introduce and consider questions related to suffering, and to draw some conclusions regarding these questions.

The leader should present a summary of the book's teaching on suffering (pages 33–39) and why some people are not healed when prayed for (chapter 8). He or she then guides the group through an open discussion based on the material covered and the discussion questions.

Discussion questions

1   The authors say the primary goal of healing is not the release from pain and sickness, it is the release from the guilt of sin. What do you think?

2   Do you know anyone who suffered from illness over a long period of time, even after being prayed for?

3   Do you know anyone who suffered from illness over a long period of time and was healed?

4   The authors suggest that the biblical idea of suffering for Christ is more concerned with suffering persecution than suffering from pain or illness. What do you think?

5   The authors write that praying for healing and growth through suffering are not mutually exclusive concepts. What do you think? (See pages 36–37.)

6   In chapter 8 the authors note four instances in the New Testament where the sick were not healed (Epaphroditus, Timothy, Trophimus and Paul). What do these exceptions tell you about divine healing?

7   Some people believe that when someone isn't healed it is because he or she lacks faith for healing. How do you respond to this idea?

8   Some people say that 'physical healing is in the atonement'. What does this phrase mean? How is Christ's work on the cross related to physical healing?

9   The authors say that scripture teaches that there is 'a time to die' and that when we pray for seriously ill people we should ask God if it is their time. What do you think of this idea?

10 Have you ever ministered to a person who was dying? What was your experience before and after his or her death?

CLINIC

The purpose of the clinic is to learn how to pray with childlike faith.

A key element of healing prayer is that we become childlike, trusting and unpretentious. Matthew 18:3–4 says, 'I tell you the truth, unless you change and become like little children, you will never enter the kingdom of heaven. Therefore, whoever humbles himself like this child is the greatest in the kingdom of heaven.' Just as earthly fathers give good gifts to their children, our Father in heaven gives 'good gifts to those who ask him' (Matthew 7:11).

All of those who would like to receive healing prayer may identify themselves. The class should break up into small groups, depending on the number of people needing healing prayer, and pray for these people. The focus of these prayers should be dependence on God and simplicity of faith: 'Father, we come before you as children, asking that you heal [name] of his/her condition. We trust you and delight in your mercy, even though we do not fully understand this situation.' Remember, 'the Lord takes delight in his people; he crowns the humble with salvation' (Psalm 149:4).

SUGGESTED BOOKS FOR FURTHER STUDY

Baker, John P. *Salvation and Wholeness*. London: Fountain Trust, 1973. (This is one of the better introductions to healing and scripture that we have seen. In chapter 3 the author, an Anglican clergyman, tackles tough questions frequently asked about divine healing. His discussions of Paul's thorn in the flesh and healing in the atonement are quite helpful.)

Clarkson, Margaret. *Destined for Glory*. Grand Rapids, MI: William B. Eerdmans, 1983. (The author, who has suffered greatly all her life, writes: 'Though I have besought God earnestly for healing, he has not seen fit to touch my body with a miracle.' This is a book of comfort.)

Cotterell, Peter. *Death*. Eastbourne: Kingsway Publications Ltd., 1979. (The author gives valuable insight from scripture to help cope with the reality of death and what lies beyond.)

Emerson, James G. *Suffering*. Nashville: Abingdon Press, 1986. (The author, a Presbyterian pastor, deals with all kinds of suffering and its possible origins. He offers a 'theology of suffering'.)

Frost, Henry W. *Miraculous Healing*. Grand Rapids, MI: Zondervan, 1979. (The subject of this book is why some people are healed and some are not.)

Graham, Billy. *Till Armageddon*. London: Hodder & Stoughton, 1982. (This book is subtitled 'a perspective on suffering'. Divine healing is not dealt with.)

Hill, Stephen. *Healing Is Yours!* Harrison, AR: New Leaf Press, n.d. (The author argues that healing is in the atonement, therefore not guaranteed to all.)

Howard, David M. *How Come, God?* New York: A. J. Holman Company, 1972. (A book on suffering, in the form of commentary on the book of Job, written by the president of the National Association of Evangelicals.)

Jeter, Hugh. *By His Stripes*. Springfield, MO: Gospel Publishing House, 1977. (The author argues for healing in the atonement.)

John Paul II. *On the Christian Meaning of Human Suffering*. Washington, DC: United States Catholic Conference, 1984. (A summary of Roman Catholic teaching on the topic of suffering.)

Kreeft, Peter. *Making Sense Out of Suffering*. London: Hodder & Stoughton, 1987. (The author is a Roman Catholic and professor of philosophy at Boston College. He writes in the style of C. S. Lewis. We believe it to be one of the finest contemporary books on suffering.)

Lewis, C. S. *The Problem of Pain*. London: Collins Fount Books, 1957. (A classic on suffering, first published in 1940.)

Murphree, JonTal. *A Loving God and a Suffering World*. Downers Grove, IL: InterVarsity Press, 1981. (This is an outstanding introduction to the broader subject of the problem of evil, of which suffering in sickness is only one aspect. Without doubt the problem of evil is the most complex question facing the Christian, and Murphree does an admirable job dealing with it.)

Tournier, Paul. *Creative Suffering*. London: SCM Press, 1982. (This is a remarkable book – well written, stimulating, sensitive. As the title implies, it describes the relationship between suffering and creativity. Especially helpful is Tournier's discussion of orphans.)

Session 3: Healing the whole person

In *Power Healing*, read chapter 4 and pages 196–197.

PURPOSE

To understand that Jesus came to heal the whole person, with spiritual healing being the key to physical and emotional healing.

READINGS

Healing is wholeness

We must remember that healing, in the Christian sense, means healing of the whole person. When we minister healing in Christ's name, we minister the whole of his redemptive love to the whole of a person's being. Our Lord's redeeming work was to free humanity from the total effect of sin, evil, and ignorance.

Reginald East

God's mercy

The order established by the Creator was indispensable to life; man's violation of it, therefore, necessarily leads to his death. But in his mercy God delays this outcome. He comes to man's aid. He heals his wounds. He protects him, in spite of himself, against the dangers into which he has run. In short, he grants him a respite, and in this respite our life is situated.

Paul Tournier

Wholeness and holiness

At the centre of the Kingdom stands the King. He alone is whole, the perfect pattern for our health. Luke, a doctor, records that at the beginning of [Jesus'] earthly life, his growth to full manhood had been in four major areas: 'Jesus increased in wisdom and in stature, and in favour with God and man' (Luke 2.52). In effect he is saying that Jesus grew mentally (in wisdom) and physically (in stature), and also spiritually (in favour with God) and socially (in favour with man). These are the four areas of growth that need to be cultivated for perfect health. When wholeness comes in these four areas, there is holiness indeed. Holiness is the goal and Jesus has revealed that holiness in all its perfection. He is the Way, the Truth, and the Life, of whose gift alone comes that wholeness and perfect health.

Morris Maddocks

DAILY SCRIPTURE READINGS

Sunday: The garden of Eden / Genesis 3:1–24
Monday: A pure heart / Psalm 51:1–12

Tuesday: Healing a paralytic / Mark 2:1–12
Wednesday: Healing at the pool / John 5:1–15
Thursday: Sanctification / 1 Thessalonians 5:23–24
Friday: Reconciliation / 2 Corinthians 5:16–21
Saturday: Life through the Spirit / Romans 8:1–16

DISCUSSION SESSION

The goal of this discussion session is to encourage the participants to compare their experience with what the authors are writing about regarding healing the whole person and the spirit.

The leader should take ten minutes to review *Power Healing*, chapter 4 and pages 196–197.

Discussion questions

1 Have you had a similar experience to Mercedes Herrera or do you know someone who has? (See pages 80–81.)
2 Have you failed many times in praying for the sick? Have you become discouraged and given up (or wanted to give up) after you tried but failed?
3 Do you know other people or have you heard of other people with dramatic stories of divine healing?
4 Have you heard stories of healing prayer within your congregation? What did you think of these stories?
5 What do you think of the idea that spiritual or psychological problems may bring on physical illness?
6 Did you have a dramatic healing when you became a Christian? Do you know someone who did?
7 Have you ever had hands laid on you when you were prayed for, or laid hands on someone else when praying for them?

CLINIC

The purpose of the clinic is to learn how to lay hands on those for whom we pray.

Touching is an intimate act that, when combined with prayer, communicates love and can be a means of communicating healing power to the sick person. Jesus frequently touched or was touched by those he healed. For example, he touched a leper (Matthew 8:2–4), touched the coffin before commanding the widow's son to rise from the dead (Luke 7:11–15), and was touched by a woman who had been bleeding for twelve years (Luke 8:43–48). The last example is of particular interest, because he observed, 'Someone touched me; I know that power has gone out from me.' Jesus regularly laid hands on the sick when he prayed for them (Mark 6:5), as did the disciples (Acts 28:8).

As a minimal goal, a person should feel loved and accepted when being prayed for. When a person is touched appropriately and affectionately, even if not healed, he or she will experience God's love.

To learn about the laying on of hands, have all those in the group who would like to receive healing prayer raise their hands. The others may gather around and lay hands on them while they pray. Here are some guidelines:

- Always ask a person's permission before laying hands on him or her.
- When possible, place your hand near the location of the hurt or suffering (in the case of physical illness), and on the head or shoulders for healing the effects of past hurts.
- For more intimate problems, such as breast or reproductive system illnesses, usually women should lay hands on women and men on men. Or a spouse may lay hands on. Alternatively they can place their own hands over the

hurt area and allow you to place your hand on top of theirs. Appropriateness is very important.

- When a small group prays, only the leader need lay hands on.
- Feelings of heat, tingling or coldness in the hands are usually an indication of the presence of healing power, though not an assurance of healing.
- Always remember this principle: It is important to treat people with respect so that they may maintain their dignity.

SUGGESTED BOOKS FOR FURTHER STUDY

Baxter, J. Sidlow. *Divine Healing of the Body*. Grand Rapids, MI: Zondervan, 1979. (One of the best introductions to divine healing written by an evangelical Protestant [Baxter is an English Baptist]. Although the book is currently out of print, the author has told us that it might be released again soon.)

Kelsey, Morton T. *Healing and Christianity*. London: SCM Press, 1973. (The author writes a scholarly and comprehensive book on the historical roots of healing. He offers helpful insights on the relationship between divine healing and medicine, psychology, and philosophy.)

Lawrence, Roy. *Christian Healing Rediscovered*. Downers Grove, IL: InterVarsity Press, 1976. (The author, a vicar of St. Stephen's in Preston, England, writes a basic introduction to divine healing.)

MacNutt, Francis. *Healing*. Tenbury Wells: Fowler Wright Books Ltd., 1974. (A classic and foundational book on healing, it offers a comprehensive look into the history of healing and the effects of world views on healing. He touches on physical healing, inner healing and deliverance.)

Maddocks, Morris. *The Christian Healing Ministry*. London: SPCK, 1981. (The author is an Anglican Bishop, and serves as Chairman of the Anglican Church's Council for Health and

Healing. His book is a defence of Christian healing, in particular arguing that Christians should proclaim the gospel of the kingdom of God and heal the sick. An outstanding book.)

Martin, Bernard. *The Healing Ministry in the Church*. Richmond, VA: John Knox Press, 1960. (This is one of the better books on divine healing, with a strong section on the healing ministry in the New Testament. It is written by a pastor of the Reformed Church, Geneva.)

Neal, Emily Gardiner. *The Healing Power of Christ*. New York: Hawthorn Books, 1972. (The author became a Christian when, as a journalist, she set out to expose 'faith healing' as a fraud [the name of her first book was *A Reporter Finds God Through Spiritual Healing*]. In this extremely well-written book Neal offers an introduction to healing. We highly recommend it.)

Needham, David C. *Birthright*. Portland, OR: Multnomah Press, 1979. (An excellent book on our identity as new creations in Christ.)

Session 4: Overcoming the effects of past hurts

In *Power Healing*, read chapter 5.

PURPOSE

To understand how experiences from our past affect us in the present, and how Christ came to heal the effects of past hurts.

READINGS

The ministry of Jesus

Modern psychiatry has proved the validity of psychiatric healing. Is it not silly to contend that Jesus healed all forms of physical diseases but did not heal the very real diseases of the inner man? Indeed, the tendency of theologians is to presume that most of the exorcisms of Jesus were psychiatric healings rather than deliverances from evil spirits. Therefore, whether the inner healing is to be found in the exorcism events or under such phrases as 'all kinds of sickness and every disease' (Matthew 4:23) or 'every sickness and every disease' (Matthew 9:35), clearly inner healings are included in the ministry of Jesus.

Michael Scanlan

Definition

I define inner healing as the healing of relationships. All healing has to do with the healing of relationships: To be fallen, as we all are, is to be separated from God, other men and women, and torn within ourselves. All people on coming to Christ need 'inner healing', or, to use a term that I prefer, prayer for personal wholeness. Christ has come into our lives, but there are large parts of us yet unconverted, unenlightened. Our souls and spirits are wounded and fragmented from having been separated from God, from having been in the clutches of the god of this world.

Leanne Payne

Confession

I have at times been accused of over-emphasizing the importance of confession, as if the whole cure of souls were contained in it. I speak from my own experience as a doctor. Without neglecting the good effects of sympathy, exhortation, advice and doctrinal teaching, I am convinced that, from a medical point of view, none of these can be compared in importance with confession.

Paul Tournier

Warning about overemphasis on inner healing

Healing of memories is a form of Christian counseling and prayer which focuses the healing power of the Spirit on certain types of emotional/spiritual problems. It is *one* and *only one* of such ministries, and should never be made the *one and only* form, for such overemphasis leads to exaggeration and misuse. It is very important that Christian workers possess both sufficient knowledge and Spirit-sensitized discernment to know when it is the right tool of the Spirit for healing.

David A. Seamands

Keeping a confidence

To be trusted not to repeat a confidence is a necessary condition of being a listener. Our attitude should be that we are in the hands of Christ, who has given us a concern for others. If our hearts are so set, not only will a breach of confidence be an abhorrence, it will cut across the nature of the call. Such a breach would be an act of self-indulgence, whereas our concern is solely for those we serve, to bring them to know the love of Christ and their fulfillment in him.

Reginald East

Ordinary people

It is a serious thing to live in a society of possible gods and goddesses, to remember that the dullest and most uninteresting person you talk to may one day be a creature which, if you saw it now, you would be strongly tempted to worship, or else a horror and a corruption such as you now meet, if at all, only in a nightmare. All day long we are, in some degree, helping each other to one or other of these destinations. It is in the light of these overwhelming possibilities, it is with the awe and the circumspection proper to them, that we should conduct all our dealings with one another, all friendships, all loves, all play, all politics. There are no *ordinary* people. You have never talked to a mere mortal.

C. S. Lewis

DAILY SCRIPTURE READINGS

    Sunday: God knows us / Psalm 139
    Monday: A new heart, a clean heart / Ezekiel 11:19–20;
                 James 4:1–10
    Tuesday: Healing a paralytic / Luke 5:17–26
Wednesday: Peter's denial / Luke 22:31–34, 54–62;
                 John 21:15–22
    Thursday: Reconciliation / Romans 5:6–11;
                 2 Corinthians 5:17–21
    Friday: The unmerciful servant / Matthew 18:21–35
    Saturday: The woman in adultery / John 8:1–11

DISCUSSION SESSION

The goal of the discussion session is to form and accept scriptural opinions about forgiveness and redemption in Christ, and apply that truth to our own lives.

The leader should take five minutes to review *Power Healing*, chapter 5.

Discussion questions

1   2 Corinthians 5:17 says, '. . . if anyone is in Christ, he is a new creation; the old has gone, the new has come!' What

does this mean for you? How do we work this out in our daily lives?

2 Read John 8:1–11. What does this story tell you about God's forgiveness? Did Jesus teach that she could continue wilfully sinning and assume God's forgiveness? How should God's forgiveness influence our willingness to forgive others who have sinned against us?

3 Read Luke 22:31–34, 54–62; John 21:15–22. Do you identify with Peter? Have you ever struggled with feelings of guilt and unworthiness such as Peter appears to have wrestled with?

4 Read Romans 5:6–11. Christianity has been called a 'bloody religion'. Why is this so, and why is the blood of Christ central to being able to live as spiritually and emotionally whole persons?

CLINIC

The purpose of the clinic is to learn how to listen to confessions and pray for forgiveness.

Galatians 6:2 says, 'Carry each other's burdens, and in this way you will fulfil the law of Christ.' The context of this passage is the restoration of a brother or sister caught in sin. James states a similar truth when he says, 'Therefore confess your sins to each other and pray for each other *so that you may be healed*. The prayer of a righteous man is powerful and effective' (James 5:16). Confession and healing go together, especially in overcoming the effects of sin and hurtful memories.

But how do we 'carry each other's burdens' and restore those who have sinned? In John 20:21–23, it says, 'Again Jesus said, "Peace be with you! As the Father has sent me, I am sending you."And with that he breathed on them and said, "Receive the Holy Spirit. If you forgive anyone his sins, they are forgiven; if you do not forgive them, they are not forgiven." ' This is a powerful passage, for Jesus teaches that in some way (surely how is a mystery) Christians experience Jesus' forgiveness through appropriate confession to their brothers and sisters. We do not imply that God forgives or withholds forgiveness of people's sins based on our pronouncements. Rather, we are the bearers of good news: that Christ's blood atones for our sins and in him we are new creations – and that to accept or reject Jesus determines forgiveness of sins.

Our point is this: Unless Jesus' forgiveness is received and believed, it is of no benefit. The emphasis is on *receiving* and *believing* forgiveness and reassurance in Christ, not on the messengers of the good news. Still, we need brothers and sisters to whom we can confess and from whom we can receive the message of forgiveness of sins.

For people to share their deepest hurts and confess, they must be assured that what they say will be held in confidence. Proverbs 11:13 says, 'A gossip betrays a confidence, but a trustworthy man keeps a secret.' Of course, there are no secrets with God, and the purpose of confessing our sins one to another is to release us from captivity to sin and guilt. So when we hear someone's confession, we are acting on behalf of God, as ambassadors of his kingdom. This means our response should be as Jesus' with the woman caught in adultery – full of compassion and mercy, yet never encouraging sin. And we should maintain their confidence as trustworthy men and women who control our tongues.

This clinic poses some challenges, because confessing sin and hurt to another person requires confidence in that person. However, this is also an excellent opportunity to clear up past wrongdoing which you have never confessed and which is holding you back from a full relationship with God. In some instances there may also be the need to extend forgiveness to others for wrongdoing done against you and which still holds you back from wholeness in Christ.

Break up into pairs with someone with whom you are comfortable. It is best for men to pair with men and women with women. Then follow these steps:

1 Pray together asking the Holy Spirit to lead your time together.

2 One of you should confess any sins that you feel need to be forgiven and discuss any other events from your past that you think might be holding you back. Only share those things that you think God is telling you to talk about; if you have no peace about sharing or nothing to share, say, 'I'm sorry, but I cannot talk now' or 'I have nothing to share.'

3 The person hearing the confession should concretely and clearly extend forgiveness in the name of Christ for all sins confessed. Say, 'In the name of Jesus Christ, your sins are forgiven. And I forgive you.' Then lead in a prayer of confession and reception of forgiveness to God. Say, 'Repeat after me: "Jesus, I am sorry for what I have done [state the sin; be specific] . . . please forgive me . . . thank you for your forgiveness." '

In some instances you will have to lead in a prayer of forgiving those who have committed sins against you (for example, a parent, spouse or friend). Again, you may say, 'Repeat after me: "Jesus, I thank you that your mercy and forgiveness even extends to [name] who sinned against me . . . I thank you that you understand my hurt and bore the pain on the cross . . . now in your name I forgive [name] . . . and I release him and my hurt to you." '

4 Now pray for the people who confessed, asking God to preserve his work of forgiveness in their lives, and asking the Holy Spirit to protect them from further satanic lies.

5 Reverse roles and repeat the process.

You may not feel comfortable with the person with whom you are paired – you may not know him or her well enough, or you may know him or her too well! Yet you may have a need to deal with sin and past hurt. If so, seek out a person in the group (or your pastor) whom you are confident you can confess to and arrange a later time to go through the steps that we have outlined here.

SUGGESTED BOOKS FOR FURTHER STUDY

Bennett, Rita. *Emotionally Free*. Old Tapnan, NJ: Fleming H. Revell, 1982. (As the title implies, this is a book about the healing of emotions. It is full of good illustrations, and easy to read.)

Dobson, Theodore Elliott. *Inner Healing: God's Great Assurance*. New York: Paulist Press, 1978. (The author, a Roman Catholic priest, uses his own life to illustrate theological and biblical principles of inner healing.)

Sandford, John and Paula. *Healing the Wounded Spirit*. Tulsa, OK: Victory House, Bridge, 1985. (This is the sequel to *The Transformation of the Inner Man*, with sections on child abuse, occult involvement, anorexia, dyslexia, schizophrenia, depression, homosexuality.)

Idem. *The Transformation of the Inner Man*. Tulsa, OK: Victory House, Bridge, 1982. (The most comprehensive book on inner healing today, it is most suitable as a resource book.)

Scanlan, Michael. *Inner Healing*. New York: Paulist Press, 1974. (Fr. Scanlan is president of the University of Steubenville, a Roman Catholic college in Ohio. The best introduction to inner healing for Christians from any tradition.)

Seamands, David. *Healing for Damaged Emotions*. Wheaton, IL: Victor Books, 1981. (A popular introduction to inner healing by a former Methodist missionary in India who is now a professor of pastoral ministries at Asbury Theological Seminary.)

Idem. *Healing of Memories*. Wheaton, IL: Victor Books, 1985. (The author continues from where he left off in his first book, *Healing for Damaged Emotions*. He lays a biblical foundation for the healing of memories and practical instruction on how to pray. It is a readable book and an excellent apologetic for inner healing.)

Tapscott, Betty. *Inner Healing Through Healing of Memories: God's Gift – Peace of Mind*. Kingwood, TX: Hunter Publishing, 1975. (Written in a simple and compassionate style, with little teaching technique. It is ideal for giving to counsellees to read as an introduction to inner healing.)

Session 5: Healing the demonised

In *Power Healing*, read chapter 6.

PURPOSE

To understand and recognise why and how demons may influence human beings today, and how in Christ we have victory over them.

READINGS

Occult bondage

Much of what is claimed as healing [by psychic or occultic healers] is probably the result of psychological rather than psychic or supernatural factors. Nevertheless, a kind of Faustian bargain takes place. Those who seek out psychic healers often come into occult bondage and become insulated against the gospel. Often those who seek physical healing in a psychic environment not only are not healed, but they are afflicted spiritually. And, of course, the very time spent with a psychic healer in long, drawn out treatments can allow the illness to reach a more serious level. Psychic healing offers one poor hope physically and no hope spiritually.

John Weldon and Zola Levitt

Giving the devil his due

Too much is being made of Satan today. What passes itself off as a renewed biblical concern for the reality of the demonic is not biblical at all. It is a negative, pessimistic message of despair that has nothing to do with the robust biblical affirmation of the superiority of Jesus over every foe we shall ever face. It is right to give the devil his due . . . but he is not entitled to overtime.

James Kallas

Spiritual warfare

One reason for increased overt activity of Satan in the lives of Christians is that until recently the subject of aggressive spiritual warfare has been largely neglected in evangelical circles. For the last seventy-five years most believers in America were lulled into an attitude of passively assuming their victory over Satan instead of aggressively applying it. When the Lord first led me into a deeper study of how the believer defeats Satan's power, I discovered that most of the sound doctrinal books written on the subject were very old. Evangelical seminaries and Bible schools had prepared their graduates to battle for the fundamentals of the faith but had provided little insight into how to engage in battle with Satan, a personal enemy.

Mark I. Bubeck

The goal of deliverance

No amount of deliverance can replace the central need in a person's life to accept the lordship of Jesus and to live out the reality of that commitment in concrete terms. Deliverance is a gift which helps men and women to live an aggressive and effective Christian life. Getting freed from evil spirits is not an end in itself, but is a means to the end. The end is union with God, life with brothers and sisters, and preaching the gospel.

Michael Scanlan and Randall J. Cirner

Prayer and inner healing

Whenever I have prayed for deliverance I have almost always also found prayer for repentance or for inner healing was necessary. Usually there is a very human weakness, such as an experience of rejection in early life, that opened the way for the demonic. Unless this deep weakness is shut off, there may be more problems later. The person is something like a tree where there has been a deep gash in the bark; if this is not covered over, the tree is always in danger of succumbing to the attack of insects or fungus which will then get within the tree and rot it out.

Francis MacNutt

DAILY SCRIPTURE READINGS

Sunday: Saul / 1 Samuel 16:14–23
Monday: Jesus' temptation / Matthew 4:1–11
Tuesday: Jesus' authority / Luke 4:31–37, 41; 6:17–19; 7:18–23; 9:37–43; 11:14–28

Wednesday: The Gerasene demoniac / Luke 8:26–39
Thursday: The authority of the Twelve / Luke 9:1,
37–50; 10:1–24
Friday: Testing the spirits / 1 John 4:1–6; 1 Peter
5:8–10
Saturday: Satan's doom / Revelation 12:7–10; 20:7–10

DISCUSSION SESSION

The goal of the discussion session is to learn more about demonic temptation, oppression and attack.

1 While it is true that Satan can tempt us (see Matthew 4:1), we are still responsible for our sin (see James 1:13–15). In other words, 'The devil made me do it' is wisdom from below. Do you agree or disagree?

2 Demons can cause disease (see Matthew 17:14–18). Do you agree or disagree?

3 Christians need not fear demons. Do you agree or disagree?

4 Christians need never fear being attacked by demons. Do you agree or disagree?

5 All mental illness is caused by demons. Do you agree or disagree?

6 Christians are called to war on the kingdom of Satan. Do you agree or disagree?

7 The fact that some Christians struggle with their full freedom in Christ may indicate they are suffering from demonic oppression. Do you agree or disagree?

8 Serious problems with relationships and constant struggles with ambition may indicate satanic influence (see James 3:13–16). Do you agree or disagree?

9 You can never trust what a demon says. Do you agree or disagree?

10 Satan's prime target is Jesus (see 1 Peter 5:8–9). Do you agree or disagree?

11 The flesh and the devil work together to tempt Christians. Do you agree or disagree?

12 Christians may be possessed by demons, to the extent that the demons have absolute control of them. Do you agree or disagree?

13 Unconfessed and serious sin is an opening to demonic influence. Do you agree or disagree?

14 Children are always protected from the influence of demons in the lives of their parents. Do you agree or disagree?

15 There is a close relationship between the occult and demons. Do you agree or disagree?

16 Living as free as possible from sin and living as consistently as possible in the power of the Holy Spirit are the best deterrents from demonic influence. Do you agree or disagree?

CLINIC

The purpose of the clinic is to learn how to exercise spiritual authority in praying for people who are tempted and afflicted by demons.

According to Luke 9:1–2, Jesus 'gave them [the Twelve] power and authority to drive out all demons and to cure diseases, and he sent them out to preach the kingdom of God and to heal the sick'. According to Acts 1:8, everyone can receive power from the Holy Spirit. Power is the ability, the strength, the might to complete a given task. But this power is of little benefit to us if we fail to use it.

Jesus said to the disciples, 'I tell you the truth, whatever you bind on earth will be bound in heaven, and whatever you loose on earth will be loosed in heaven' (Matthew 18:18; see also 16:19). By this he meant the authority to announce guilt or innocence in his name, not to determine guilt or innocence in our own authority. He was saying that we have been given his authority, but we must exercise it to experience it.

Effective prayer for people struggling with demonic temptation, oppression and attack, or for people suffering under the guilt of serious and unconfessed sin, involves binding and loosing. Sometimes this comes in the form of a simple declaration upon hearing someone's confession of sin: 'In the name of Jesus, I tell you that you are forgiven and Satan has no authority to lie to you and tell you that you are guilty.' For habitual problems caused by demonic influence or attack, we have the authority to restrain and silence demons. Again, this authority may be expressed through a simple statement: 'In the name of Jesus, I bind any evil spirit who may be harming [name]. You may no longer lie to him/her or bring him/her down. Now be gone!'

We have discovered that yelling at the devil is less effective than quietly praying to God. While yelling may scare the person for whom we are praying, only Jesus' power frightens demons. We must always keep in mind that we are Jesus' ambassadors, so we speak with his authority and power. The demons must obey, for Jesus is Lord of the universe.

Anyone who suffers chronically from troublesome dreams (the kind that awaken you with fear or perverse thoughts) or unnatural temptations (such as sudden desires to sin that periodically come on you) should raise his or her hand. The larger group should break up into small groups, designate group leaders and pray for the people struggling with troublesome dreams and unnatural temptations. After interviewing the person to discover what he or she needs prayer for, the group should lay hands on the person and speak with Jesus' authority to any demonic influence that they sense is present, or extend forgiveness in the case of repentant sin.

SUGGESTED BOOKS FOR FURTHER STUDY

Bounds, E. M. *Satan: His Personality, Power, and Overthrow*. Grand Rapids, MI: Baker Book House, 1972. (A classic, nineteenth-century book on the devil.)

Bubeck, Mark I. *Overcoming the Adversary*. Chicago, IL: Moody Press, 1984. (An excellent study of the armour of God as described in Ephesians 6. The author outlines four keys to victory over Satan: union with Christ, the Holy Spirit, the armour of God and the 'all-ness' of prayer.)

Harper, Michael. *Spiritual Warfare*. London: Hodder & Stoughton, 1970. (One of the best books written on spiritual warfare. The first part describes the battle, the second part tells how we win in Christ.)

Kallas, James. *The Real Satan*. Minneapolis, MN: Augsburg Publishing House, 1975. (The author traces the concept of the devil from both the Old Testament and the New Testament, demonstrating that Christians have been given power to overcome any of his attacks.)

Koch, Kurt E. *Between Christ and Satan*. Grand Rapids, MI: Kregel Publications, 1961. (The majority of the book describes – from a Christian standpoint – such practices as fortune-telling, magic, spiritism and occult literature. Chapter 6 contains sixteen case studies of deliverance and healing.)

Idem. *Demonology, Past and Present*. Grand Rapids, MI: Kregel Publications, 1973. (A book of outlines from talks that Dr Koch has delivered in seminaries and Bible colleges all over the world. Especially helpful to Christian counsellors who encounter the demonic in people.)

Lewis, C. S. *The Screwtape Letters*. London: Collins Fount Books, 1977. (An excellent book for anyone who questions the existence of the devil and demons, first published in 1942.)

Montgomery, John Warwick, ed. *Demon Possession*. Minneapolis, MN: Bethany Fellowship, 1976. (A collection of papers presented at the University of Notre Dame in 1975 under the auspices of the Christian Medical Society.)

Nevius, John L. *Demon Possession*. Grand Rapids, MI: Kregel Publications, 1968. (Originally published in 1894, this is an evangelical classic on demon possession. The author was a Presbyterian missionary in China.)

Newport, John P. *Demons, Demons, Demons*. Nashville, TN: Broadman Press, 1972. (Subtitled 'a Christian guide through the murky maze of the occult', this volume is well written and researched.)

Russell, Jeffrey Burton. *Satan: The Early Christian Tradition*. Ithaca, NY: Cornell University Press, 1981. (This scholarly book describes what the early church fathers as far as the fourth century believed about Satan.)

Scanlan, Michael, and Randall J. Cirner. *Deliverance from Evil Spirits*. Ann Arbor, MI: Servant Books, 1980. (This is the best introduction to the deliverance ministry that we know of. We recommend it highly to all Christians.)

Shiels, W. J. *The Church and Healing*. Oxford: Basil Blackwell, 1982. (This is a compilation of papers written for the British Ecclesiastical History Society. Especially interesting is 'Doctors, Demons, and Early Methodist Healing', by Henry D. Rack.)

Tozer, A. W. *I Talk Back to the Devil*. Edited by Gerald B. Smith. Harrisburg, PA: Christian Publications, 1972. (This little collection of Tozer sermons is sure to jolt the reader out of spiritual indifference.)

Unger, Merrill F. *What Demons Can Do to Saints*. Chicago, IL: Moody Press, 1977. (Perhaps the best book out on the question, 'Can a Christian be indwelt by a demon?')

Session 6: Healing the body

In *Power Healing*, read chapter 7.

PURPOSE

To understand the complex relationship between the soul, mind and body, and how Christ heals the body today.

READINGS

Jesus' concern for physical wellbeing

It was Dr. Albert Schweitzer who once remarked that his only purpose with regard to disease was to annihilate it. In this he was remarkably at one with his Master's thinking. Jesus' one objective was the elimination of disease and the restoration of man to wholeness. This fact makes the attitude of the medieval church little short of a tragedy, for it was Jesus of Nazareth and Lord of the Church, more than any other religious leader, who showed the greatest concern for the physical and mental well-being of man.

Morris Maddocks

Modern medicine and divine healing

Sometimes it is forgotten that medicine owes its greatest debt not to Hippocrates, but to Jesus. It was the humble Galilean who more than any other figure in history bequeathed to the healing arts their essential meaning and spirit . . . Physicians would do well to remind themselves that without his Spirit, medicine degenerates into depersonalized methodology, and its ethical code becomes a mere legal system. Jesus brings to methods and codes the corrective of love without which true healing is rarely actually possible. The spiritual 'Father of Medicine' was not Hippocrates of the island of Cos, but Jesus of the town of Nazareth.

J. W. Provonsha, MD

Prayer for physical healing

Although prayer for physical healing may stretch your faith (have you ever prayed for a blind person?), it is also the simplest kind of prayer. It is much simpler and shorter, say, than a prayer for inner healing.

Francis MacNutt

Assuming on God

The Christian is entitled to bring all problems, including health, in prayer to God, but is not entitled to lay down what particular answer he should give, or at what time.

We can make bold and specific requests as long as we do so 'if it is thy will'.

Rex Gardner

Prayer

Some of the most wonderful healings on record, and some of the most wonderful healings that I have known in my own body and in the bodies of others, have been in answer to the prayers of the one who was sick, entirely without the help of others.

R. A. Torrey

DAILY SCRIPTURE READINGS

Sunday: Naaman healed of leprosy / 2 Kings 5:1–27
Monday: Hezekiah's illness / 2 Kings 20:1–11
Tuesday: Healing on the sabbath / Luke 14:1–6
Wednesday: The faith of the centurion / Matthew 8:5–13
Thursday: Healing a deaf and mute man / Mark 7:31–37
Friday: Paul heals a crippled man / Acts 14:8–20
Saturday: The prayer of faith / James 5:13–16

DISCUSSION SESSION

The goal of the discussion session is to talk about various issues raised in chapter 7 of *Power Healing*. (The discussion questions are drawn from the text.)

Discussion questions

1 Are you sceptical when you hear reports of divine healing of physical problems like cancer?

2 Do you believe it is more difficult to forgive sins than heal physical illness? (See Matthew 9:1–8.)

3 What was your response to Dr Friend's account of the healing of baby Tina on pages 143–145?

4 Do you know anyone who has been healed of a functional disorder? What was the illness? How was he or she healed?

5 What was your response to D. M.'s healing on pages 145–147? Do you understand how the Holy Spirit used his mental images of Vietnam to aid the healing process?

6 Some people think all divine healing is only a form of psychological healing that in turn affects physical health. How do you respond to this notion?

7 Some people believe divine healing precludes modern medicine. They even imply that if a person receives healing prayer, he or she should not see a physician. What do you think?

8 Whose faith – that of the person praying or the sick person's – is most important in healing prayer?

9 Have you ever experienced the sensation of something like spiritual power going out from you when you prayed over someone for divine healing? (See Mark 5:25–34.)

10 In Mark 7:31–37, Jesus healed a deaf and mute man by putting his fingers in the man's ears, then spitting and touching the man's tongue. Have you ever seen or heard of someone being healed through unusual means?

11 Francis MacNutt points out that most people are totally healed only after several sessions of prayer (he calls this soaking prayer – see also Mark 8:22–26). Do you know of anyone who was healed through soaking prayer?

CLINIC

The goal of the clinic is to pray for those who have been partially healed.

All those who have been partially or totally healed during the previous five clinics should share their testimonies with the rest of the group. Then those who have been partially healed and others with physical ailments may receive healing prayer in small groups.

SUGGESTED BOOKS FOR FURTHER STUDY

DiOrio, Ralph A. *Called to Heal*. Garden City, NY: Doubleday & Company, 1982. (The author, a Roman Catholic priest, is founder and director of the Office of the Apostalate of Prayer for Healing. In this book he reflects on his call to pray for the sick, and presents a number of reports from persons who have claimed healings.)

Frazier, Claude A., editor. *Faith Healing: Finger of God? or Scientific Curiosity?* Nashville, TN: Thomas Nelson Publishing, 1973. (The editor, a physician, asked twenty Christian doctors to present papers on faith healing. Their conclusions are mixed, though some leave room for divine healing. The weakest chapters are where the physicians attempt to be biblical scholars or church historians. They would have done well to have kept to their field of expertise.)

Pitts, John. *Faith Healing: Fact or Fiction*. Westwood, NJ: Fleming H. Revell, 1961. (The author, who believes in divine healing even though he is confined to a wheelchair, argues that medical doctors and clergy should work together.)

Reisser, Paul C., Teri K. Reisser, and John Weldon. *The Holistic Healers*. Downers Grove, IL: InterVarsity Press, 1983. (A Christian perspective on the New-Age health care movement. Unfortunately, the book is out of print.)

Weldon, John, and Zola Levitt. *Psychic Healing*. Chicago, IL: Moody Press, 1982. (The strength of this book is its fine analysis of psychic healing and the occult. Unfortunately, the authors do not offer much practical help for those caught up in psychic healing, nor do they offer much commentary on 'divine healing.)

Wilkinson, John. *Health and Healing*. Edinburgh: The Handsel Press, 1980. (A scholarly study of New Testament principles and practice of healing. An outstanding resource for the serious student of divine healing.)

Session 7: An integrated model of healing

In *Power Healing*, read chapters 9 and 10.

PURPOSE

To introduce the principles, values, practices, programmes, and personnel of the healing model.

READINGS

A corporate responsibility

The ministry of healing is not merely the vocation of a small minority with successful experience in this field, but belongs to the overall pastoral ministry of the clergy. Neither is the ministry of healing a clerical prerogative, but a corporate responsibility for the whole church. A happy development in the healing ministry has been the growing awareness that the entire local community is called to minister to the needs of the sick through prayer or intercession groups, by visiting the sick, and by displaying the understanding and acceptance of the sick person.

Charles W. Gusmer

Sharing in Christ's ministry

Everything that has been made is made to be something which expresses God, and so men are made for life, and for fulness of life, and by the power of Christ's redemption – by bringing harmony into their lives once again – they can be healed. And so our Lord told his disciples to go out and heal the sick; to have fellowship with him in his work of restoration. That is the ministry of the church in which we have a part. I believe that the whole church is meant to be the fellowship of those who, with Christ, work for his purpose of the redemption of the world, and that we can have and should take our share in that work of healing.

Jim Wilson

Doubt

There is a wise old proverb: 'If in doubt, don't.'

It is not the duty of every Christian to pray for everyone. Our prayers will help some and will not help others, for reasons beyond our understanding or control. Only the Holy Spirit can safely direct our healing power. And if we will listen to the voice of God within, we will be shown for whom to pray. God directs us most joyfully through our own desires. The impulse of love that leads us to the doorway of a friend is the voice of God within, and we need not be afraid to follow it. The impulse of love will also direct our words. The one who goes to a sorrowing friend in the spirit of love will not make the mistake of saying, 'I feel that it is my duty to come to see you.'

Agnes Sanford

Wyclif on healing

John Wyclif, in the first extant English translation of the New Testament, for the Greek word *soteria*, which we normally translate 'salvation', rendered 'health'. So he has Paul telling the Roman Christians that he is not ashamed of the gospel because it is 'the virtue of health for believers'. Wyclif was obviously on to something: it has taken us a long time to catch up.

Rex Gardner

DAILY SCRIPTURE READINGS

Sunday:	Jairus' daughter healed / Mark 5:21–24, 35–43
Monday:	The Syrophoenician woman / Mark 7:24–30
Tuesday:	The sending out of the Twelve / Matthew 10:1–42
Wednesday:	Pentecost / Acts 2:1–42
Thursday:	Tabitha raised from the dead / Acts 9:36–43
Friday:	Eutychus raised from the dead / Acts 20:7–12
Saturday:	Spiritual gifts / 1 Corinthians 12:1–13:13

DISCUSSION SESSION

The goal of the discussion session is to evaluate your personal attitudes towards the practice of healing prayer, and the attitudes and practices of the larger Christian group to which you belong.

You should each take five minutes to think about the following questions, then divide into small groups of four or five and discuss your answers.

Part 1: Your personal attitudes

1 Do you believe that God heals today?
2 Do you believe that every Christian can learn to pray for the sick?
3 Do you believe that every Christian is empowered by the Holy Spirit to pray for the sick?
4 Do you believe that loving relationships are a goal and effective environment for healing?
5 Do you believe that it is more important to learn about the person than a particular illness when praying for the sick?
6 Do you believe that an atmosphere of faith, hope and acceptance is important when praying for the sick?
7 Do you believe that worshipping God increases faith for healing?
8 Do you believe that occasional failures are normal when praying for the sick, especially when learning how to pray?
9 Do you believe that teams are usually more effective than individuals at praying for the sick?
10 Do you believe that you are called to pray for the sick in situations other than in Christian meetings, such as in homes, on the streets and at work?
11 Do you believe that it is important to hear God's voice when you pray for the sick?
12 Do you believe that it is possible to see (spiritually) the Holy Spirit coming upon someone?

13 Do you believe that the laying on of hands is an important part of healing prayer?
14 Do you believe that any Christian, if they have faith for healing and openness to God's healing power, can heal the sick?
15 Do you believe that all the spiritual gifts described in the Bible are available to you?
16 Do you believe that gifts other than gifts of healing – for example, words of knowledge or discerning of spirits – are important when praying for the sick?
17 Do you believe that some Christians have been called to train others to pray for the sick?

Part 2: Your church's attitudes

Consider the above questions again, only this time examine the prevailing attitudes in the church of which you are a member. For example, question 1 would be: 'Does your church believe that God heals today?'

CLINIC

The goal of the clinic is to introduce the group to the five-step healing procedure described in *Power Healing*, chapters 11 and 12.

In the last three clinics you will be praying over the sick using the five-step method. In this clinic the leader, who will have already read *Power Healing*, chapters 11 and 12, will give a brief (ten minute) summary of the method.

SUGGESTED BOOKS FOR FURTHER STUDY

Archbishops' Commission. *The Church's Ministry of Healing*. Church House, Westminster: The Church Information Office, 1958. (This is a report from the Anglican Archbishops' Commission on healing, in which they endorse the church's ministry of healing. The commission offers a number of recommendations for healing practices in the Anglican church.)

Beckmen, Richard J., and Stephen J. Nerheim. *Toward a Healing Ministry*. Minneapolis, MN: Augsburg Publishing House, 1985. (An excellent introduction to divine healing for Lutherans. The authors include suggested liturgies appropriate for the Lutheran church.)

Bennett, George. *The Heart of Healing*. Valley Forge, PA: Judson Press, 1971. (Written by an Anglican hospital chaplain, this book is subtitled 'A Handbook on Healing'. It is an excellent introduction to divine healing for members of mainline Protestant and Catholic churches.)

East, Reginald. *Heal the Sick*. London: Hodder & Stoughton, 1977, (A solid book whose aim we heartily endorse: 'to encourage Christians, ordained and lay, in local churches to take the healing ministry into their system'. This is a practical volume.)

Gunstone, John. *The Lord is Our Healer*. London: Hodder & Stoughton, 1986. (The author demonstrates the relationship between the ministry of healing and spiritual renewal in the local church – especially in historic denominations; the author is an Anglican priest.)

Gusmer, Charles W. *The Ministry of Healing in the Church of England: An Ecumenical-Liturgical Study*. Great Wakering, Essex: Mayhew–McCrimmon, Ltd., 1974. (One need not be an Anglican to gain much from this book, though a good portion of it concerns healing and the Anglican liturgy. The section entitled 'Common Misconceptions About the Church's Ministry of Healing' is excellent.)

Robins, Henry Charles. *A Guide to Spiritual Healing*. London: A. R. Mowbray & Co., Ltd., 1953. (This short [99 pages] book, written by a Church of England cleric, is quite practical and easy to read. It is especially helpful for those from liturgical traditions.)

Session 8: A healing procedure, part 1

In *Power Healing*, read chapters 11 and 12.

PURPOSE

To introduce the group to the five-step method for healing prayer, particularly the interview and diagnostic decision steps.

READINGS

A good beginning

We remind the people who participate in prayer-counseling at our seminars that those four days of meetings with 'in-service training' of actually praying with people do not make them fully equipped but are a good *beginning*. We encourage them to study, pray, and grow in their knowledge and skill, while remaining under the leadership of their pastor and participating in the church family.

Rita Bennett

Take your time

Because the prayer session is so important, it is essential that it be planned properly. The session requires *unhurried time* and *an unpressured schedule*. This means that it should not simply be an hour worked into a regular counseling schedule. It should not be subject to clock-watching by anyone. The pastor or counselor should not be anxious about some other person impatiently waiting for an appointment, or a committee meeting that is about to begin.

David A. Seamands

Correct diagnosis

Just as in medicine doctors often fail in diagnosing diseases and consequently fail to prescribe the right medicine and treatment, so the minister of healing, if he lacks discernment, is bound to fail from time to time.

Francis MacNutt

DAILY SCRIPTURE READINGS

Sunday: Answered prayer / 1 John 5:13–15; Matthew 18:18–20
Monday: The blind man at Bethsaida / Mark 8:22–26
Tuesday: Jesus heals a man born blind / John 9:1–41
Wednesday: Healing a boy with a demon / Matthew 17:14–21
Thursday: Peter heals the crippled beggar / Acts 3:1–4:22
Friday: The slave girl at Philippi / Acts 16:16–40
Saturday: Paul on Malta / Acts 28:1–10

DISCUSSION SESSION

The goal of the discussion session is to answer questions that arise in people's minds about their experience in praying for the sick, and especially about the five-step method of prayer.

The leader should devote thirty minutes to overseeing an open discussion concerning observations, questions and complaints regarding the participants' experience during the previous seven weeks in praying for the sick both inside and outside the clinics.

Special attention should be devoted to different areas in need of healing:

- The spirit;
- The effects of past hurts;
- Demonisation;
- Physical illness.

CLINIC

The purpose of the clinic is to learn how to interview and make a correct diagnosis in praying for the sick.

The leader should call for someone who needs healing prayer. Then, with the group watching, the leader can take the person through the five steps, stopping frequently during the interview step to explain why he or she is asking certain questions or making certain comments.

The leader should then describe what he or she thinks the root of the person's problem is and how that analysis was arrived at. Steps three, four and five – prayer selection, engagement and post-prayer direction – do not need the detailed explanation of the first two steps; they will be discussed in detail next week.

The group may then break up into smaller prayer groups to pray for those needing healing, using the five-step model.

A special note to leaders

In preparation for sessions nine and ten, you should contact your pastor and ask for a list of people in hospitals, old people's homes or at home who need healing prayer. If your pastor does not know of anyone, contact another pastor in your area. The number of people needed will be determined by the size of the group. Be sure to get their names, conditions, addresses and phone numbers. (For more details, see the clinic section in session nine.)

SUGGESTED BOOKS FOR FURTHER STUDY FOR SESSIONS 8, 9 AND 10

Bennett, Rita. *How to Pray for Inner Healing for Yourself and Others.* Old Tappan, NJ; Fleming H. Revell, 1984. (Probably the most practical book on inner healing today. It outlines different ways of praying, areas where difficulty is normally encountered, and how to begin a prayer ministry in the local church.)

Glennon, Jim. *Your Healing Is Within You.* London: Hodder & Stoughton, 1978. (A good introduction to the healing ministry in the New Testament. It includes an especially helpful section on the 'prayer of faith'.)

Hagin, Kenneth E. *Understanding the Anointing.* Tulsa, OK: Rhema Bible Church, 1983. (This is one of the few books we have come across on the anointing of God. The author deals with individual anointing, anointing of ministry gifts, and corporate anointing.)

Koch, Kurt E. *Charismatic Gifts.* Quebec, Canada: The Association for Christian Evangelism, 1975. (An excellent section on the discerning of spirits and its relationship to revivals. Sketched from a historical perspective.)

Kuhlman, Kathryn. *I Believe in Miracles.* London: Lakeland Books, 1968. (Twenty-one dramatic and authentic cases of healing.)

Lawrence, Roy. *Invitation to Healing.* Eastbourne: Kingsway Publications, 1979. (In this book the author offers practical advice for praying for the sick. His discussion of death, particularly a chapter in which he recounts the story of one man coming back from the dead, is excellent.)

MacNutt, Francis. *The Prayer that Heals.* London: Hodder & Stoughton, 1982. (Subtitled 'Praying for Healing in the Family'. The author offers practical insight for how to pray for and with those whom we love most.)

Payne, Leanne. *The Broken Image.* Westchester, IL: Crossway Books, 1981. (The author is an Episcopalian laywoman who emphasises healing of the whole person, with special insights into problem areas of human sexuality. Her chapter on 'Listening for the Healing Word' is excellent. Her case histories are very helpful.)

Idem. *Crisis in Masculinity.* Westchester, IL: Crossway Books, 1986. (Probably the best book available on praying for those suffering from homosexual neuroses. The case histories make the book come alive.)

Idem. *The Healing of the Homosexual.* Westchester, IL: Crossway Books, 1984. (This little book is the best introduction we know of for inner healing of homosexuals.)

Idem. *Real Presence.* Westchester, IL: Crossway Books, 1979. (Subtitled 'The Holy Spirit in the Works of C. S. Lewis', this is the author's first book.)

Torrey, R. A. *Divine Healing.* Grand Rapids, MI: Baker Book House, 1974. (A classic monograph by the former superintendent of Moody Bible Institute. Of particular interest is his discussion of James 5:14–15.)

Tournier, Paul. *A Doctor's Casebook in the Light of the Bible*. Trans. by Edwin Hudson. Crowborough: Highland Books, 1983. (This book, written by a Swiss physician, is worth the price for part 3, 'Life, Death, Disease, and Healing'.)

Session 9: A healing procedure, part 2

In *Power Healing*, review chapter 12 and read Appendix E.

PURPOSE

To introduce the group to steps three, four and five of the five-step method for healing prayer: prayer selection, prayer engagement and post-prayer direction.

READINGS

Ministry

Ministry to another must always be a fresh meeting in the presence and power of the Lord and by His leading. Our participation in that encounter is primarily to connect the person with Jesus, and to participate with Him in enabling the person to recognize and eliminate the blocks (at whatever level) to the life the Lord would lavish upon him in love. Patterns to look for in people's lives and ways to deal with them must always be submitted to the present moving of the Spirit or we will unwittingly attempt to 'use' God to accomplish what we mistakenly perceive to be 'our' ministry, and manipulate the other person by a technique we have developed.

Paula Sandford

By my Spirit, says the Lord

When we pray with the sick, we keep attentive to the Spirit. Should a vision be given, we describe it. If a prophecy or word of knowledge or wisdom, we speak it out. We then act upon what is said. So the Spirit will guide the form and content of our prayer. It may happen that there is no strong lead from the Spirit. In that case we pray as it seems right in the circumstances. As we have already committed ourselves into the Spirit's hands, we can be confident that it is still he who is making our prayer.

Reginald East

Who can pray?

A truth that surprises many Christians when they first hear it is that each of us has the gifts of healing and prayer right now. Yes, it is true. Each of us has all the gifts of the Holy Spirit (enumerated by St. Paul in 1 Corinthians 12:4–11) and have had them since we were baptized. The gifts of the Spirit are our birthright as children of God, our inheritance from the Father . . . The Holy Spirit, as one of the three Persons of the Trinity, is divinely simple – he is infinite and indivisible. He cannot give part of himself, for he is not in parts. Therefore when he comes to a person in baptism he brings all of himself and all of his gifts, including the gifts of prayer and healing.

Theodore Elliott Dobson

Prayer

According to Saint Teresa of Avila, 'There is but one road which reaches God, and that is prayer.'

This is, of course, true, but prayer is not only the road to God. It constitutes the very atmosphere we breathe in the climate of healing; it is the oxygen of the spirit. It is the means by which we are enabled to live continually in that relationship.

Emily Gardiner Neal

DAILY SCRIPTURE READINGS

Sunday: Our weapons / Ephesians 6:10–18
Monday: Sobbing / Nehemiah 8:1–12
Tuesday: Hannah appears drunk / 1 Samuel 1:1–20
Wednesday: Daniel trembles, falls over / Daniel 10:1–19
Thursday: Praise / Luke 17:11–19
Friday: Thrown to the ground / Mark 9:14–32
Saturday: Clean house / Matthew 12:43–45

DISCUSSION SESSION

The goal of the discussion session is to answer questions that arise in people's minds as they compare their experience in praying for the sick with what they read in *Power Healing*.

The leader should devote thirty minutes to overseeing an

open discussion concerning observations and questions regarding the participants' experience in the previous clinic, and to reviewing the phenomena that occur among people in response to God's power and truth (see *Power Healing*, chapter 12).

CLINIC

The purpose of the clinic is to learn how to make a correct prayer selection, engage in prayer and bring post-prayer direction.

The leader should call for someone who needs healing prayer to be prayed over. Then, with the group watching, the leader can take the person through the five steps, stopping frequently during the prayer selection, engagement and post-prayer direction in order to discuss in detail what he or she is doing.

Of particular concern is learning to see the Holy Spirit when he comes on people – the signs of his power and presence – and learning how to bless his work.

In preparation for next week, divide into groups of two or three people. The leader will then assign to each group two people in nursing homes, hospitals or at home who need healing prayer. Each small group should assign a facilitator to arrange a time to pray with the sick person during the following week. The leader should take a few minutes to review Appendix E, 'Healing Those in Hospitals'.

Before leaving, the group may then break up into smaller prayer groups to pray, using the five-step model, for those needing healing.

Session 10: A healing lifestyle

In *Power Healing*, review chapters 11 and 12.

PURPOSE

To understand and commit yourself to a lifestyle of healing.

READINGS

Sharing ministry

It takes courage for a pastor to let people begin sharing in the ministry in such things as prayer-counseling. More and more, the minister is realizing, though, that he can't possibly meet the needs of the congregation, seeing them in church only a few hours each week, and there just isn't enough of him to go around, even for those who are brave enough to ask for personal attention.

Rita Bennett

The church: Christ's body on earth

The Church's ministry of healing is the ministry committed to the Church by our blessed Lord himself – and the
Church in its widest sense is the family of all Christian
souls. The Church was meant by Christ to be the body
through which he would carry on his work in the world.
He lived in the world, and he carried on his ministry of
healing and preaching. Then men nailed to the cross the
hands that had been laid upon the sick. They silenced the
tongue that had spoken the words of healing. The feet
upon which he had walked about doing good were nailed
and helpless. From that moment he had no body through
which to work, until he formed his Church and sent it
into the world to be his new body through which he
would lay his hands on the sick, through which he would
teach men, and through which he would go about doing
his work.

Jim Wilson

Progressive faith

Though divine healing may be immediate, its progressive
character should be clearly understood. We need to keep
in mind two things said by our Lord: firstly, that healing
is part of the kingdom of God; and secondly, that the
essential nature of the kingdom is to grow. This means
that healing can come like the growing of a plant;
minutely small at first, but in the long run full-grown.

Jim Glennon

More and less

The most important thing I have learned in the past few

years about praying for healing is that *usually* people are
not completely healed by prayer, but they are *improved*.

Francis MacNutt

DAILY SCRIPTURE READINGS

   Sunday: Psalm 32
   Monday: Psalm 4
  Tuesday: Psalm 38
Wednesday: Psalm 41
 Thursday: Psalm 103
   Friday: Psalm 147
 Saturday: Isaiah 52:13–53:12

DISCUSSION SESSION

The goal of the discussion session is to learn from the small
groups' field experience during the past week.

Discussion questions

1 What did you do to prepare yourself for the prayer
   time?
2 How would you describe the atmosphere in the place
   that you prayed? Fearful? Full of faith? Sceptical?
3 Did the person for whom you prayed have faith for
   healing?
4 Did you have faith for healing?
5 Did you read any scripture?
6 How did the interview go?

7   Did you have a problem making a proper diagnosis?
8   What did you pray? Did your prayer confirm that your
    original diagnosis was correct, or did you have to
    change your prayers?
9   How long did you pray?
10 Did you know when to stop praying?
11 How did you work together as a team?
12 Were your prayers answered?

CLINIC

The purpose of the clinic is to pray for those who feel called
to a healing lifestyle.

If the group is part of a larger church congregation or
parish, and the pastor is not participating in the study, the
leader should meet with the pastor to discuss how healing
prayer may be made available to any church member
through mid-week gatherings or after Sunday services. If
the pastor endorses a healing prayer ministry in the church,
and if he approves of group members' involvement in that
ministry, the leader should use the clinic hour to organise
and call for commitment to pray for the sick in the church.

In closing, the group should break up into small groups
consisting of three to five people and pray for each other,
that the Lord may bless each person to live out a healing
lifestyle.

Our prayer for you is this:

Father, we pray that you bless all that you have done in
the lives of every person who participated in this study.
For those who were healed, we pray that you would
protect them from their condition returning, and that you
would give them boldness to tell others of your grace. For
those who were not healed or were only partially healed,

we pray that through continued prayer they may be completely healed. For those who have begun praying for the sick, cause their faith to increase and use them in healing many in the years to come. For those who still have questions, give them answers so that they may become more effective vessels of your compassion and mercy. And for everyone in the study we pray that what they have learnt changes the way they live. Amen.

Appendix A: Tips for leaders

If you have only casually glanced at the material in this book, no doubt you have noticed that our goal is twofold: to learn more about divine healing and to learn how to pray for the sick. For most of you, leading a discussion about divine healing is a great challenge; leading a group of people who are actually to pray for the sick seems impossible! You might be tempted to withdraw before you start. Leading people into the practice of divine healing *is*, humanly speaking, impossible. But with God 'all things are possible' (Mark 10:27).

Over the years we have led many small groups and classes. Here are a few tips from our experience that will help you in the discussion and clinic sections.

PREPARATION

Your personal preparation is the most critical element for success. Prayer is the starting-point here. I can think of no other activity in the Christian life that is more dependent on God's grace than divine healing. The daily scripture readings should be springboards for intercession. We suggest that you pray for every participant by name.

Many leaders struggle with feelings of inadequacy: they think that they do not know enough and are not able to answer all the questions that arise. Well, be assured that you will not be able to answer all the questions that arise, so put that concern aside. But if you diligently study *Power Healing* and this study guide you will be more than adequately equipped to lead the discussion and clinic sessions. A thorough familiarity with everything written in the book and guide will prepare you for most questions that arise during the course of the study. For those questions you cannot answer, we suggest you respond as we do: 'I don't know.'

THE DYNAMICS OF GROUP DISCUSSION

Small group discussion about healing usually raises many strong opinions and emotions. Few people are neutral about the subject. Because of this, you need an awareness of the dynamics of group discussion.

Many people will enter the study group having had bad experiences with praying for the sick, experiences that created great doubt and scepticism about divine healing. They may have lost an immediate family member after praying for his or her healing. They may have attended a healing conference in which the healer acted in a bizarre manner. They themselves may have received healing prayer, but with no results. These people need the freedom and opportunity to talk about such experiences and work them through. This means you need patience and a loving heart to not only hear what they say but feel what they feel.

There may be other people who are quite positive about divine healing. Perhaps they or a loved one have been healed. Or perhaps their reading of scripture has led them to conclude that healing is for today. In some instances these people develop unrealistic expectations, equating God's work in divine healing with his work of forgiveness. They believe healing should always be immediate and one hundred percent, and if it is not, something is wrong. They will tend to make grandiose claims and encourage inappropriate beliefs.

If leaders allow these two groups (the sceptics and the 'true believers') to dominate the discussion, they will severely polarise the group. Polarisation usually means paralysis; the group as a whole will not learn. This means one must not allow people with dogmatic opinions – either for or against divine healing – to control the group. When someone talks too much or with an inappropriate attitude, I usually try to talk with him or her privately, asking them to help make room for others in discussion. Also, we suggest several of the discussions be conducted in groups of two to four, thus assuring that everyone can be heard. People need the opportunity to discuss and digest the ideas in a learning atmosphere.

CLINIC

Most churches offer few courses that combine the theory and practice of some discipline of the Christian life. They do not require immediate behavioural changes. But this course has as one of its major objectives the learning of a new skill – how to pray for the sick.

This means that you must encourage participants to come as learners. I usually begin each clinic session with a learner's prayer: 'Lord, we are here to learn from you. We want to become like you. It is our desire to live as the apostles lived, to be a people who demonstrate your kingdom with words and works.'

People do not advance in understanding and aptitude at the same rate. Their understanding usually runs ahead of their ability to perform. So the practice of praying for the sick will lag behind the understanding. This means that the discussion sessions may be more dynamic (especially in the first three or four sessions) than the clinic sessions. But the clinic sessions soon catch up with the discussions, usually becoming the most exciting part of the study by sessions nine and ten.

Most Christians are not too familiar with the intimate dialogue and the practice of laying on hands that are an integral part of praying for the sick. In a ten-week course, this means that even conducting a clinic is a major accomplishment. The very activity of attempting to pray for the sick is success, because as people become accustomed to listening to God's voice, intimate conversation with others, laying on hands, intercession and petition – all the elements of healing prayer – those skills are gains in themselves, regardless of whether or not someone is healed!

So the highest value in the clinic is not that you see someone healed, it is that you persevere in healing prayer. As leaders you should encourage the people to continue the activity of healing prayer, because as they gain ability in these different areas they move closer to effective healing prayer.

Learning to pray for the sick in a group is very important. Why? Because if only one person prays successfully the entire group experiences success.

Praying for the sick is both exhilarating and frightening. Exhilarating, because every Christian wants to please God and advance his kingdom. Frightening, because divine healing is supernatural and challenges Western cultural values of materialism and rationalism. So it is necessary to recognise that if you struggle with the feelings of excitement and fear, most of the other people in the group will be feeling the same emotions.

People moving into fearful situations are often helped when they have clearly defined expectations, limitations set on what practice and behaviour is expected of them. These expectations create a secure learning environment and provide criteria for evaluating success or failure. The best way to create appropriate expectations is to stay within the confines of scripture and good sense, boundaries that the book and guide are intended to provide.

They also must be assured that learning to pray for the sick takes time, that it cannot be learnt overnight. The ministry of healing is for every Christian and it's natural for God to do the supernatural. God is committed to us when we commit ourselves to pray for the sick. But sometimes he must do work in us before he can more effectively work through us. As the leader you help others persevere through their failures by demonstrating and encouraging courage and trust.

Appendix B: Sources for chapter readings

CHAPTER 1

Francis MacNutt, *The Power to Heal*. Notre Dame, IN: Ave Maria Press, 1977, p. 149.

A. B. Simpson, *The Gospel of Healing*. Harrisburg, PA: Christian Publications, 1915, p. 6.

Donald Bloesch, from unpublished notes, 1984.

CHAPTER 2

A. J. Gordon, *The Ministry of Healing*. Harrisburg, PA: Christian Publications, 1961, pp. 235–236.

Margaret Clarkson, *Destined for Glory*. Grand Rapids, MI: William B. Eerdmans, 1983, p. 132.

Jim Glennon, *Your Healing Is Within You*. London: Hodder & Stoughton, 1978, pp. 178–179.

Peter Kreeft, *Making Sense Out of Suffering*. London: Hodder & Stoughton, 1987, pp. 149–151.

CHAPTER 3

Reginald East, *Heal the Sick*. London: Hodder & Stoughton, 1977, pp. 12–13.

Paul Tournier, *A Doctor's Casebook*. Trans. by Edwin Hudson. New York: Harper & Row, 1954, pp. 165–166.

Morris Maddocks, *The Christian Healing Ministry*. London: SPCK, 1981, p. 16.

CHAPTER 4

Michael Scanlan, *Inner Healing*. New York: Paulist Press, 1974, p. 11.

Leanne Payne, 'Making Sense Out of Sexual Identity', *Commonlife* (Fall 1986). Mansfield, OH, p. 2.

Paul Tournier, *A Doctor's Casebook*. Trans. by Edwin Hudson. Crowborough: Highland Books, 1983, p. 209.

David A. Seamands, *Healing of Memories*. Wheaton, IL: Victor Books, 1985, p. 24.

Reginald East, *Heal the Sick*. London: Hodder & Stoughton, 1977, p. 88.

C. S. Lewis, 'Weight of Glory', *Transposition and Other Addresses*. London: Geoffrey Bles, 1949, pp. 32–33.

CHAPTER 5

John Weldon and Zola Levitt, *Psychic Healing*. Chicago, IL: Moody Press, 1982, p. 234.

James Kallas, *The Real Satan*. Minneapolis, MN: Augsburg Publishing House, 1975, pp. 12–13.

Mark I. Bubeck, *Overcoming the Adversary*. Chicago, IL: Moody Press, 1984, p. 14.

Michael Scanlan and Randall J. Cirner, *Deliverance from Evil Spirits*. Ann Arbor, MI: Servant Books, 1980, p. 3.

Francis MacNutt, *Healing*. Tenbury Wells: Fowler Wright Books Ltd., 1974, p. 229.

CHAPTER 6

Morris Maddocks, *The Christian Healing Ministry*. London: SPCK, 1981, p. 163.

J. W. Provonsha MD, 'The Healing Christ', in *Current Medical Digest* (December 1959), p. 3.

Francis MacNutt, *Healing*. Tenbury Wells: Fowler Wright Books Ltd., 1974, p. 192.

Rex Gardner, *Healing Miracles*. London: Darton, Longman and Todd, 1986, p. 206.

R. A. Torrey, *Divine Healing*. Grand Rapids, MI: Baker Book House, 1974, p. 47.

CHAPTER 7

Charles W. Gusmer, *The Ministry of Healing in the Church of England: An Ecumenical-Liturgical Study*. Great Wakering, Essex: Mayhew–McCrimmon, Ltd., 1974, p. 55.

Jim Wilson, *Healing Through the Power of Christ*. Cambridge: James Clarke & Co., Ltd., 1946, pp. 12–13.

Agnes Sanford, *The Healing Light*. Evesham, Worcestershire: Arthur James, 1969, p. 112.

Rex Gardner, *Healing Miracles*. London: Darton, Longman and Todd, 1986, p. 64.

CHAPTER 8

Rita Bennett, *How to Pray for Inner Healing for Yourself and Others*. Old Tappan, NJ: Fleming H. Revell, 1984, p. 29.

David A. Seamands, *Healing of Memories*. Wheaton, IL: Victor Books, 1985, p. 139.

Francis MacNutt, *Healing*. Notre Dame, IN: Ave Maria Press, 1974, p. 254.

CHAPTER 9

John and Paula Sandford, *Healing the Wounded Spirit*. Tulsa, OK: Victory House, 1985, p. xviii.

Reginald East, *Heal the Sick*. London: Hodder & Stoughton, 1977, pp. 64–65.

Theodore Elliott Dobson, *Inner Healing: God's Great Assurance*. New York: Paulist Press, 1978, pp. 61–62.

Emily Gardiner Neal, *The Healing Power of Christ*. New York: Hawthorn Books, 1972, p. 105.

CHAPTER 10

Rita Bennett, *How to Pray for Inner Healing for Yourself and Others*. Old Tappan, NJ: Fleming H. Revell, 1984, p. 103.

Jim Wilson, *Healing Through the Power of Christ*. Cambridge: James Clarke & Co., Ltd., 1946, p. 7.

Jim Glennon, *Your Healing Is Within You*. London: Hodder & Stoughton, 1978, p. 170.

Francis MacNutt, *The Power to Heal*. Notre Dame, IN: Ave Maria Press, 1977, p. 27.